In celebration of:

_____

Thoughts:

Name:

Thoughts:

Name:

Thoughts:

Name:

Thoughts:

Name:

Thoughts:

Name:

Thoughts:

Name:

Thoughts:

Name:

Thoughts:

Name:

Thoughts:

Name:

Thoughts:

Name:

Thoughts:

Name:

Thoughts:

Name:

Thoughts:

Name:

Thoughts:

Name:

Thoughts:

Name:

Thoughts:

Name:

Thoughts:

Name:

Thoughts:

Name:

Thoughts:

Name:

Thoughts:

Name:

Thoughts:

Name:

Thoughts:

Name:

Thoughts:

Name:

Thoughts:

Name:

Thoughts:

Name:

Thoughts:

Name:

Thoughts:

Name:

Thoughts:

Name:

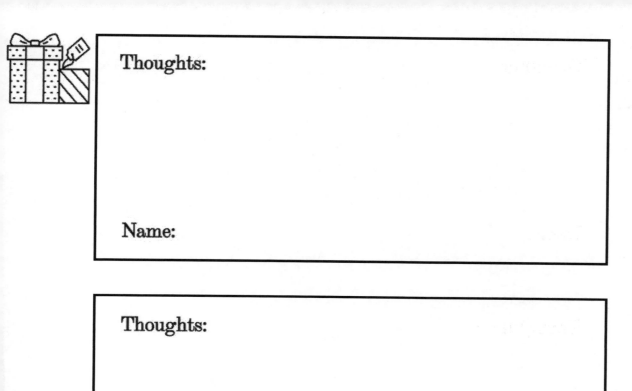

Thoughts:

Name:

Thoughts:

Name:

Thoughts:

Name:

Thoughts:

Name:

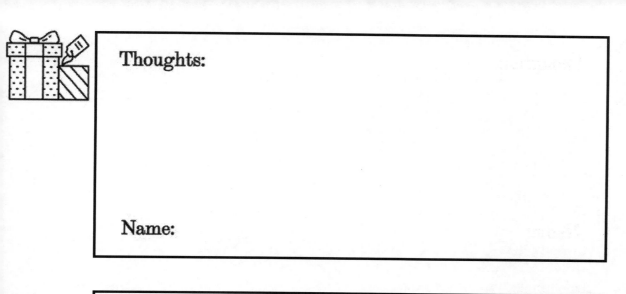

Thoughts:

Name:

Thoughts:

Name:

Thoughts:

Name:

Thoughts:

Name:

Thoughts:

Name:

Thoughts:

Name:

Thoughts:

Name:

Thoughts:

Name:

Thoughts:

Name:

Thoughts:

Name:

Thoughts:

Name:

Thoughts:

Name:

Thoughts:

Name:

Thoughts:

Name:

Thoughts:

Name:

Thoughts:

Name:

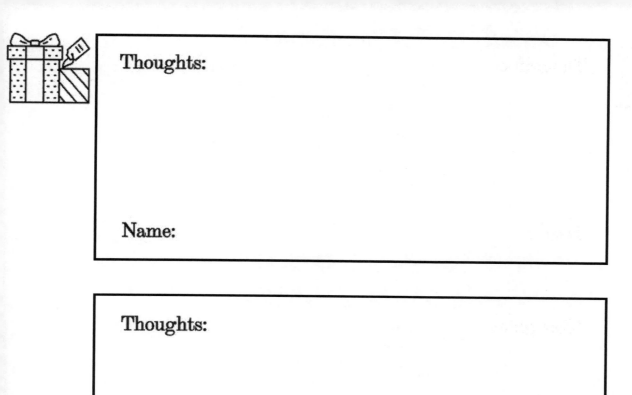

Thoughts:

Name:

Thoughts:

Name:

Thoughts:

Name:

Thoughts:

Name:

Thoughts:

Name:

Thoughts:

Name:

Thoughts:

Name:

Thoughts:

Name:

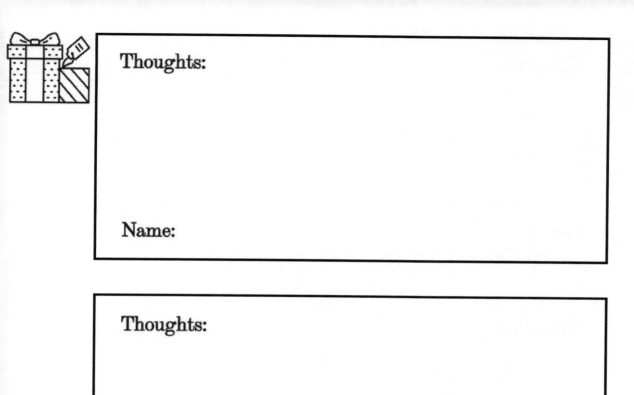

Thoughts:

Name:

Thoughts:

Name:

Thoughts:

Name:

Thoughts:

Name:

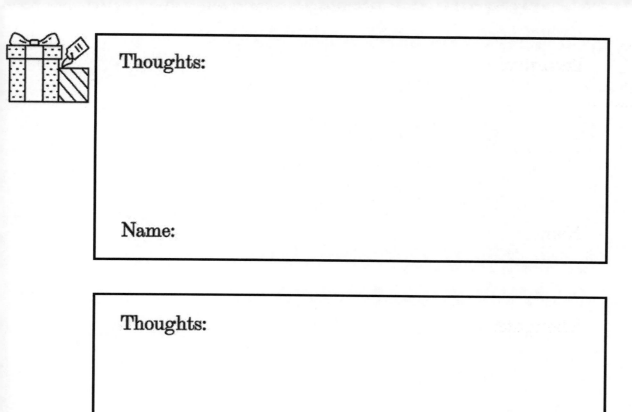

Thoughts:

Name:

Thoughts:

Name:

Thoughts:

Name:

Thoughts:

Name:

Thoughts:

Name:

Thoughts:

Name:

Thoughts:

Name:

Thoughts:

Name:

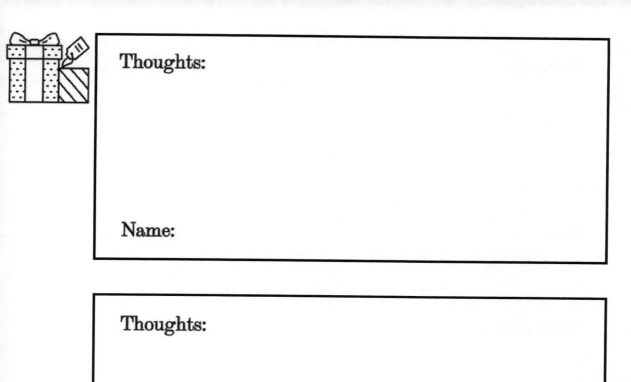

Thoughts:

Name:

Thoughts:

Name:

Thoughts:

Name:

Thoughts:

Name:

Thoughts:

Name:

Thoughts:

Name:

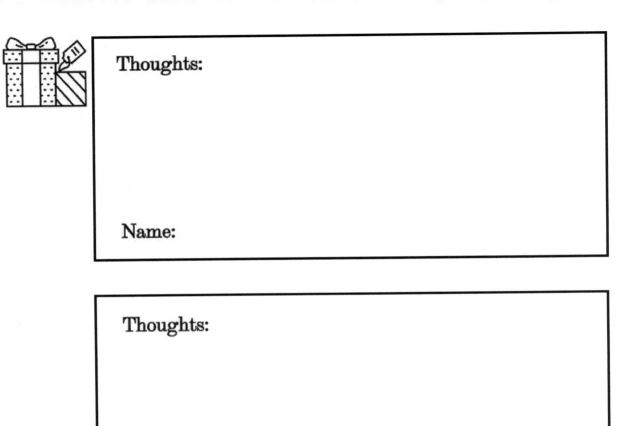

Thoughts:

Name:

Thoughts:

Name:

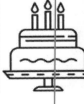

Thoughts:

Name:

Thoughts:

Name:

Thoughts:

Name:

Thoughts:

Name:

Thoughts:

Name:

Thoughts:

Name:

Thoughts:

Name:

Thoughts:

Name:

Thoughts:

Name:

Thoughts:

Name:

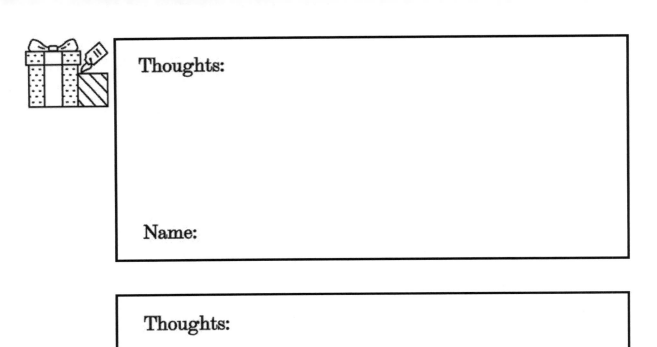

Thoughts:

Name:

Thoughts:

Name:

Thoughts:

Name:

Thoughts:

Name:

Thoughts:

Name:

Thoughts:

Name:

Thoughts:

Name:

Thoughts:

Name:

Thoughts:

Name:

Thoughts:

Name:

Thoughts:

Name:

Thoughts:

Name:

Thoughts:

Name:

Thoughts:

Name:

Thoughts:

Name:

Thoughts:

Name:

Thoughts:

Name:

Thoughts:

Name:

Thoughts:

Name:

Thoughts:

Name:

Thoughts:

Name:

Thoughts:

Name:

Thoughts:

Name:

Thoughts:

Name:

Thoughts:

Name:

Thoughts:

Name:

Thoughts:

Name:

Thoughts:

Name:

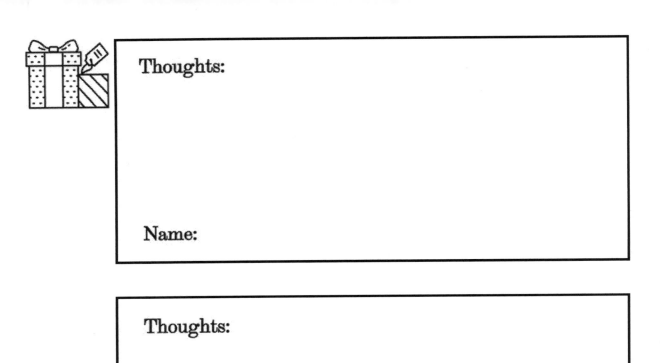

Thoughts:

Name:

Thoughts:

Name:

Thoughts:

Name:

Thoughts:

Name:

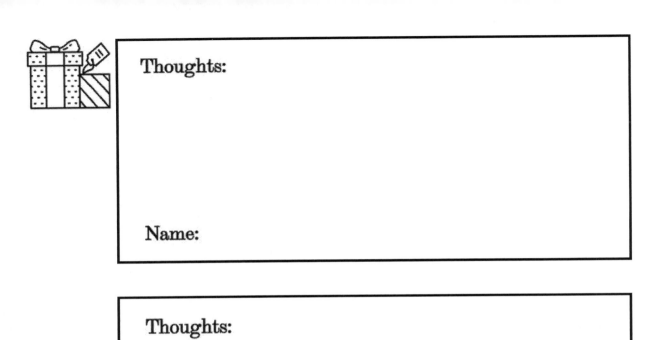

Thoughts:

Name:

Thoughts:

Name:

Thoughts:

Name:

Thoughts:

Name:

Thoughts:

Name:

Thoughts:

Name:

Thoughts:

Name:

Thoughts:

Name:

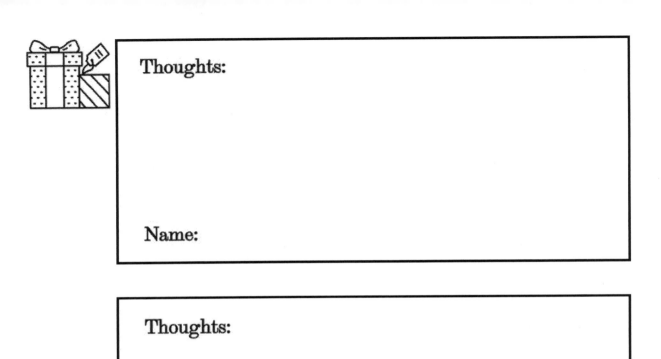

Thoughts:

Name:

Thoughts:

Name:

Thoughts:

Name:

Thoughts:

Name:

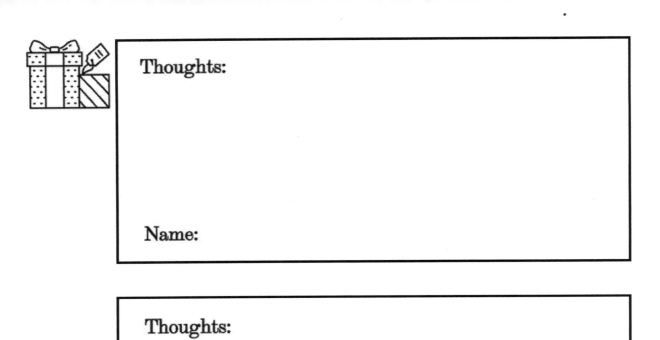

Thoughts:

Name:

Thoughts:

Name:

Thoughts:

Name:

Thoughts:

Name:

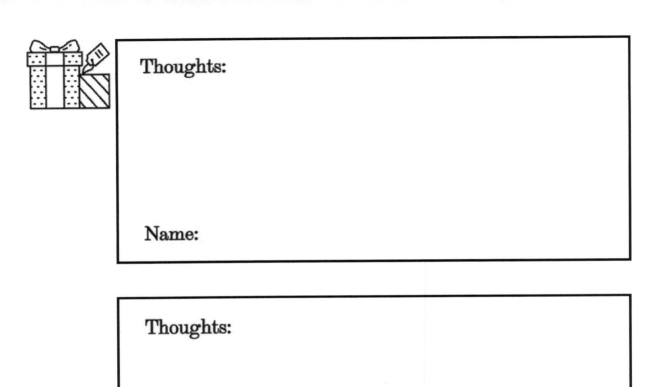

Thoughts:

Name:

Thoughts:

Name:

Thoughts:

Name:

Thoughts:

Name:

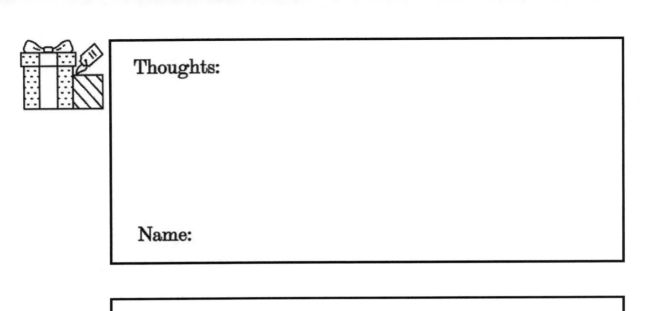

Thoughts:

Name:

Thoughts:

Name:

Thoughts:

Name:

Thoughts:

Name:

Thoughts:

Name:

Thoughts:

Name:

Thoughts:

Name:

Thoughts:

Name:

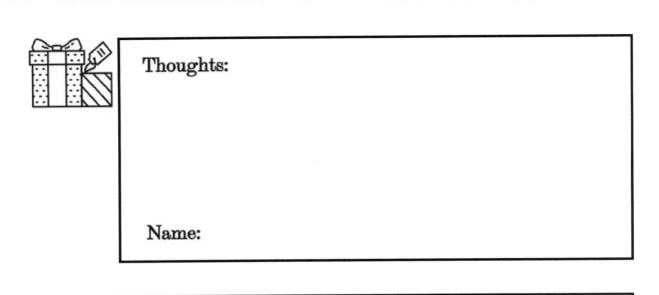

Thoughts:

Name:

Thoughts:

Name:

Thoughts:

Name:

Thoughts:

Name:

Thoughts:

Name:

Thoughts:

Name:

Thoughts:

Name:

Thoughts:

Name:

Thoughts:

Name:

Thoughts:

Name:

Thoughts:

Name:

Thoughts:

Name:

Thoughts:

Name:

Thoughts:

Name:

Thoughts:

Name:

Thoughts:

Name:

Thoughts:

Name:

Thoughts:

Name:

Thoughts:

Name:

Thoughts:

Name:

Thoughts:

Name:

Thoughts:

Name:

Thoughts:

Name:

Thoughts:

Name:

Thoughts:

Name:

Thoughts:

Name:

Thoughts:

Name:

Thoughts:

Name:

Thoughts:

Name:

Thoughts:

Name:

62159994R00057

Made in the USA
Middletown, DE
22 August 2019